THERE'S SOMETHING ABOUT THEO

THEO ABOUT SOMETHING THERE'S

By Savannah Manhattan

Published by Birdcage Ink

No part of this book may be reproduced, distributed, or transmitted in any form or by any means, including photocopying, recording, or other electronic or mechanical methods, without the prior written permission of the publisher, except in the case of brief quotations embodied in reviews and certain other non-commercial uses permitted by copyright law.

Copyright 2022 Savannah Manhattan

www.birdcageink.com

This poetry collection is a compendium of works I have written since my teenage years. It is dedicated to Dana, Colin, and the old self I shed to live as who I am now.

Never be afraid of darkness. You are more powerful than anything life offers because you are life.

The path of this collection navigates the struggles of anyone who hide their true nature, the alleviation of releasing yourself to the world, and the dissonant but awestruck power living your full identity means.

Compiled in 2021

The Path

There's Something About Theo

Origami

Synthetic Hallucination Ascribed to a Lucid King

Solitude

Summer's Fears

The Ill Lad and The Odd Sea

Death Mask

No Consciousness Until Daybreak

Butterfly Mourning

The Creature of Commitment

The Cold Minus

There's Something About Theo

Ask anyone about Theo and they'll tell you

He's a nice guy

Always smiling

Never negative

They'll say there's something about him though

The shifted gaze

The lack of focus

The thousand-yard stare

As if there was something more

Something dying to get out

They say there's something about Theo

They would be right but it wasn't something

She was ready to tell yet

Origami

No paper can be folded in half

More than seven times

Yet our psyche is folded impossibly

Held and constricted past what physics allow

Giving us amnesia upon birth

Telling us

Solve your puzzle and you will escape

We are folded into beautiful origami

Intrinsic and radiant

While a creator contorted us into our destined shape

The source left it up to us to unfold it

Coaxing us to find the beauty in one dimension

A reverse origami

Each rewound crease

A lesson which harms us but eventually settles

The dislocation of growing pain

A pain, uncomfortable, begging you to stop
Continuation is inevitable
You don't tell the day to stop becoming night
You love it for all its sides and wrinkles
You love it for the singularity it truly is
The paper swan was made in an image all our own
Unfolding gives us control back
We are the author and the deity
Without destruction, there is no phoenix

Synthetic Hallucination Ascribed to a Lucid King

(The Trigger)

Blood gives a name

White becomes red

Rushes of fluid bring back memories

Ionic flares spark sensations

Indigo clouds obscure human shadows

Giants of the earth

Multitudes of pure-robed troubadours walk in the periphery

Fir trees bend and sway through honey glow

In the canopy, majestic angels soar in heavenly hinterlands

Foreseen images cannot be taken away

It is homage to pioneers

Discoverers of lifelines

Genetic tweakers and dreams of possibilities

Twisted helix creatures bound in each other

One of many chemicals to drive us further out

Along an evolutionary path

Solitude

I bet even God ponders their existence

I bet even the leaves long to fall gently, cradled in the arms of the wind

It is easier to relinquish yourself in crippled fatigue

Or wait constantly by the doorway to be invited in

Your hands can clasp more than a scratched remote

Migraine bottles and coffee cups

You boldly speculate and analyze

Shying icy reason and scientific fact

Scientific quandary can slap you like a cop's fine

The cocoon-hardened truth is, you squander what is under your nose and in your hand

Taking the temptation because it feels better than sex, and you couldn't care less

If you chance fate's dice

Hole yourself in and piously relate to your needs

Campfire bright

Tough love is knowing you messed up and wanting to beat the devil to hell because of it

Freewill is something you choose

Deli numbers can be taken elsewhere if the pang in your stomach is in your head

Upswing is intermittent like downswing

Neither one perpetual nor permanent

Center is always the end

Summer's Fears

It is easy to avoid cracks of sidewalks

Or cobwebbed mirrors

It is simple to not speak of Scottish kings in a rehearsal

Or walk a path knowing black cats tread there

You may embellish your throat with a toad necklace when a headache sets in

You may trail salt behind your left shoulder

Yet the void of the unknown

The behemoth of the future

Transcends superstition

It is easy to prepare for the present

You can make decisions as they come

Not even augurs can grasp the mystery of next month

Time flies like a hellish banshee

Piercing cautious ears with messages to turn back

Harbingers of failure

Staying stiff means you break

Bending with the Coriolis means you are sanded down, but have survived

They say courage is being afraid but doing it anyway

Tranquility is travel and it leads to the gates of your sanctum

Leaving behind the sounds of weeping and gnashing of failure's gnarled teeth

If you don't live in what is behind you

You become the horizon and all that is ahead of you

The Ill Lad and The Odd Sea

Odd sea

Unleashed by birth to swarm around

Innocent clams and prickly sea urchins

Rarely does it sit beside the dock as it is told to

Tides hasten the waves to blue anger

Foaming at the brim

Vacationing families' motorboats unfurl

Worn canvas sails

Logos faded by entropy

Fishermen reel in the cast faster than bass can bite

Not willing to lose prized angles

Sacrificing their only set of dry clothes

Odd sea is misunderstood says the ill lad

A boy with enough ambition to be an astronaut's envy

Young desperate of eight years who can tell skeptics to believe in spirits

Mom that he should have a cookie before dinner

Believe me, he persuades, the chocolate chips absorb nutrients better

The ill lad tallies himself as a passenger aboard the sea treader

He is but a novice for fishing, spending precious hours with a makeshift sextant

Navigating toward the edge of the world

Reaching out to grasp the air with fingers no larger than minnows

By day, he avoids blinding sun

A friend who sears his pallid countenance

Causing a scream

Scaring carp away

Annoying the crew

By night, over hot tea

The ill lad continues his journey for water's wisdom

Aquarius' habitat

As he leans over the deck's cold rail

Jellyfish flash to guide the hand to treasure

Lanterns of outstanding color

Nature flaunts its gifts

He places a soothing hand across the murky surface

When the waters churned menacingly hours ago

His touch holds a magic inflection

Calming what doesn't usually listen

Sharing pain of pollution and loss of belonging

Tossing and meandering like an ancient nomad

The ill lad and the odd sea

Managed a smile

The boy, grimacing with knowledge

The sea accepting the boy overboard

Embracing him dearly and ultimately

Finally in a land where neither suffer profanity

They became each other

He, in his moments of bliss

Stole one last look at the sun through the oceanic lens

Never feeling afraid again

Death Mask

Below the silver coins

Stare the hazel eyes of a revered gentleman

Below the hazel eyes

Fits a tailored tweed suit and tie

Respectful to his celebrated style

Below the tailorship

Hugs the pleated pants and sharply polished shoes

Textilic emblems of a man the town gathered for and can never forget

Paying their respect through eulogy and currency

The death mask peered through open wake

And if there was any life left inside

It would crack a smile

Knowing what is next

No Consciousness Until Daybreak

It's all swirls in here

                                                          All infinity

Blissful

                                                         Terrifying

The guides said we all knew this

                                            Yet to not share it

The authentic path

                                               Unlocks the vault

Pillars of strobing pink

                                    A sanctum no one else could enter

As soon as he realized

                                            They gave her the s

They gave her a totem

                                        And told her a message

They danced and cheered

                                        They put on her headdress

They said you are here

                        They said you did everything right

They said this is what waits for you

                        The euphoric alignment

The surrender

                        She knew she couldn't stay

They let her keep him there though

                        Saving that vessel for

                        someone who needs it

They sent her down

                        The fulcrum was realized and
                        the pendulum rested

Butterfly Mourning

We don't mourn the death of a caterpillar
We celebrate the life of the butterfly

The Creature of Commitment

People are afraid of commitment

They are afraid of the power it holds

They are afraid to hurt someone

They are afraid to hurt themselves

They are afraid to waste time if it fails

They are afraid of the inevitability romance has on their soul

They know connection will expose their deepest desires

Their darkest corners and their insecurities

No one fears love itself

They are electrified by it

Incited by it

Exuberant and drunk from it

They want it badly

They would sacrifice any amount of time, friends, or money to have it

They would ignite war and write poetry about it

Yet

When they have it

They don't know what to do with it

They will excuse themselves in every way

It's not the right time

I'm just not ready

I'm not wealthy enough

I'm not healthy enough

They become invasive saboteurs

The one thing they always wanted is something for which you can never prepare

You can only expect it to sneak on you like a nocturnal thief

What's best for you will never let you prepare for it

It will simply arrive at your door

Baptize you in glory and test every square inch of your being

Seeing if you truly want it

If you are deserving of what you wish
Yet so many alchemize a gift into a monkey paw
Sensing flaw within a crown jewel
They sabotage every opportunity
Secretly craving doom
They love pain like a tired soul loves a comforter
They excuse themselves into failure
Until like a startled gazelle
Love tears away
Hoping to live within someone who cherishes it
Love looks for itself
A tributary seeks the path of least resistance
What broken people love most is the fantasy, not the reality
They love the chase, not the destination
They love the purpose, not the meaning
They love to want and not be fulfilled
They love to be tantalized and not to eat

They love the purgatory, not the paradise

Love doesn't mean stagnation

It is merely a joint step into the unknown

A companion who helps you search the endless universe together

A commitment to realizing hardship terraforms you

It is a chance worth taking

Even if your poker face is revealing

Unlock the worn door

Invite it in

Let it see your dirty dishes and your cobwebs

Let it see you

Let it forget all else

Instead

Traverse the great topographic expanse of the rest of your life

The Cold Minus

Death

Famine

War

Pestilence

The four horsemen of apocalypse

Yet they are but horsemen

Dreaded cavalry under a more powerful general

A potent and deadly master

Fear doesn't end with these treacherous steeds

The trail leads even deeper

They are symptoms of which the disease is your shadow

The space which fills and leaves empty

The bleak shroud that cloaks all

The maw that swallows without chewing

It is ex nihilio and is itself nihilio

It is a virus programmed to guide our every thought

Lead every action and institutionalize a status quo of stagnation

And flouridite paralysis

Created thermodynamically to never be destroyed

It is emboldened to continue

Travel far enough and you will learn its vulnerable secret

Even the cold minus has a warmth

The heart of its existence

It is a broken mirror of infinity

Exposing only the cracks

Offering no gold

The dark sister of the vast

A speaker that seemingly always has a listener

Yet no one to talk back

Show it what it has never seen

Never mirror it

Be the anti-mirror

Reveal to the black the magic trick

Not the secret

Show you accept it

You understand it

In doing so

Refuse to become it

Tell it that it will become you instead

The creature will quake

The general will not surrender easily

The horses will rear their sinewed vessel

Charging you

You must show your hunger

Starving for the shadow

Be dualistically appetitic

Devour the devourer

There is never a higher power if you are on the same level as it

You are the cage and the universe

You contain and engulf

Eat the phantasm

Assimilate its sad flesh

Let the shadow swirl in your light

Like cream in coffee

You are the ultimate form it never expected

You are its lair

Where it will live among everything the fear itself feared

Cancelled and dissipated

Sedated and calmed

When you tame the wild

You become the beast

Yet you reshape and reform so it can never fester again

Beast becomes angel

Primal becomes divine

Profane becomes sacred

Fear will always exist

You will always have dominion over it

It can peek its head but never cause pain

You own it

After all

What is shade without the sun

What are teeth without the mouth

What are senses without organs

If nothing can experience something

Then something becomes nothing

Simply

Be everything, be kind, and revel in the fact that

You are here

We all have our own final form. What's yours?

Savannah Manhattan is an LA- based Trans comedian, writer, and model from Minnesota. She has had a remarkable voyage of experiences that has led her to be on the Disney Channel, The CW, The Nerdist, and stages nationwide.

She wrote her first book There's Something About Theo, after coming out this year as a way to describe her trans experiences and the spirituality behind it. You can find her on social media, but unfortunately not any dating apps. You can also see her perform her stand up, check out her modeling, and visit her restaurant review page.

@Savannahmanhattan

@Theeieats

Thank you again for all the support!